Gravities: Insights and Emotions in Verse, Second Edition

Levities and Gravities, Second Edition, Volume 2

Benjamin Cannicott Shavitz

Published by Benjamin Cannicott Shavitz, 2023.

While every precaution has been taken in the preparation of this book, the publisher assumes no responsibility for errors or omissions, or for damages resulting from the use of the information contained herein.

GRAVITIES: INSIGHTS AND EMOTIONS IN VERSE, SECOND EDITION

First edition. June 20, 2023.

ISBN: 979-8223580461

Written by Benjamin Cannicott Shavitz.

Table of Contents

For Beauty

INTRODUCTION

This volume is a collection of poems written in a serious tone. It is part of the author's Levities and Gravities project. The Levities and Gravities project demonstrates the power of linguistic form in poetry and highlights the fact that poetry can evoke any emotion, whether light or heavy. This volume contains "gravities," or serious poems, but the companion volume, *Levities*, presents humorous poems. This second edition contains additional poems not included in the first edition, new author's notes, and an essay on the possibilities available in poetry.

THE AUTHOR

Benjamin Cannicott Shavitz holds an M. A., an MPhil, and a PhD in linguistics from The City University of New York and previously taught The Structure of Modern English and The History of the English Language at Hunter College in Manhattan, New York City. Since linguists understand language to be the pairing of form and meaning, Ben's poetry engages not only with meaning but with the aspects of linguistic form, including prosody (meter), phonological patterns (e. g., rhyme, alliteration, sound class patterning), and translanguaging and dialectal phenomena (e. g., varying and mixing dialects and languages). Ben's training in the structure of language affords him technical control over the form of his poems, allowing for infinite design possibilities. Ben also holds a B. A. in multidisciplinary studies from Stony Brook University, which covers concentrations in engineering, English, and linguistics, as well as peripheral studies in numerous other areas. Ben's broad knowledge base fuels the subject matter of his poems, so he writes on a wide range of topics. Ben's poem "Before the Fall" (not included in the Levities and Gravities series) is set to be published in an upcoming edition of the poetry magazine *The Lyric*. Ben was born in 1993 in Manhattan, New York City where he still resides. For more of Ben's work and poetry, view www.kingsfieldendeavors.com[1].

---

1. http://www.kingsfieldendeavors.com

#Me

Who someone is is who they are,
Not what they're forced to tag themself.
It's every hope and skill and scar,
Not pre-fab labels off the shelf.

I cannot understand my soul
By framing it in terms of yours.
I answer to the cosmic whole,
Not search terms that the wind ignores
And drowns when, on a whim, it roars.

A Grand Utility

All art is found unjustified in light of artists' needs.
A usefulness is lacking there to pay each resource back.
But impact grants to symbols greater weight than goods or deeds,
A grand utility that cost-effective products lack.

Allegiance

Why do humans love their mothers
When existing is to suffer?
Parents force us into being.
Should we not prefer our brothers
Who provide our greatest buffer,
Easing life that could be rougher,
So we don't depart by fleeing?
Comrades help us leave existence
Having offered it resistance.

Anger

Anger is the sword of feeling.
Grief will wield it wanting fairness.
Fear will wave it wide for spacing.
Joy will slash at competition.

Swords, however, owe no kneeling
Fealty to a lord, awareness-
Lacking as they are, embracing
Masters with a worthy mission.
Anger's blade will serve ambition.

Anticipation: March 15th

I can hear them all sing
The beginning of spring,
All the breezes and birds,
From the sky, on the wing.
And the absence of words
Has a curious ring
Since the message is clear:
That the moment is near —
Something bright and absurd's
Rising out of the year,
Spread with frivolous hues,
All a peacockish thing.
It's about to appear.
And the pleasantest news
Is they say it has something to bring.

Apathy

The world has pulled me in too deep
And, since I somehow never weep,
The only thing to do is sleep.
But, someday, I, like all, will die
And maybe then I'll get to cry,
Although there'd scarce be reason why.

Arizona

I hardly find it fair to say
That sanity is sane,
When normal minds will daily pray
For unresponding rain
To fertilize the arid clay
That forms the desert plain,
Upon which they insist they'll stay,
And starve on dead terrain.

Avian Philosophy

I asked of a falcon
That sat on a balcony
Tearing the guts from a pigeon,

"Ma'am, how do you silence
The qualms about violence,
Infixed into every religion?

The avidest birder
Still disesteems murder
What quiets your doubts? What's the teaching?

Can man square compunction
With natural function?"
The falcon responded by screeching.

Babble's Birds
(A Collection of Indo-European Techniques)

The most ancient of arts I aim
To revive so its voice prevails
As a beacon of beauty based
On wingèd words.

So I've pulled from the poets past
All the forms that feed phonic flash
And I've stocked them inside my sack
Of babble's birds.

Author's Note: This poem uses a meter that has been reconstructed as being typical of the poetry of the Indo-Europeans, the linguistic ancestors of a very large portion of the human population. This poem also uses assonance (rhyming of vowels that does not necessarily involve the matching of the consonants that follow the vowel), alliteration, rhyme (matching of both vowels and the consonants that come after them), and the phrase "wingèd words," all of which have been used in the poetry of one or more Indo-European groups. For more information on these issues of form, see *Indo-European Poetry and Myth* by M. L. West.

Better Days

The motherland was perfect.
We feel this for a certain fact.
For there we still were people
And held the pride of place we've lacked.

But there we still were people
And people everywhere must hate.
When everything was perfect,
What humans did *we* deprecate?

Betwixt Two Selves

There is a beast supporting all of us,
The baseness that will be the fall of us,
The chaos that creates a squall of us.
It slavers in the grime.

But there is too a god of each of us
That ever sits above the reach of us
And when we warrant any speech of us,
It is because we climb.

Beyond the Myopia of Sorrow

There's more to life than what you see.
A new world waits beyond that tree.
Revival sits behind that rock
And if upon that door you knock,
It will swing in to let you through
To lands thick tears now hide from view.

So hasten now: rise up, stand tall
And you will see beyond that wall
A life that now seems quite unreal
Because of how I know you feel,
A world in which you'll hear and see
The children laugh with raucous glee,
A life in which your soul is fresh
And dwells again within your flesh.

Just peer behind that stone or tree.
For though it lies across a sea,
If you can pass beyond its post,
You will no longer be a ghost.
You will be flesh and blood again.
You will rejoin the world of men.

So have some faith, and keep in mind
The world remains, to which you're blind.
Just know that once you've scaled the wall
That stands cloud-high and will not fall,

You'll gaze upon a land still there
Where songbirds flutter through the air.
There lies a world beyond that gate
And it's not leaving. It will wait.

Camelot

Society's an upward-growing tower and its destiny's to fall.
But, someday, if we're ardent, archaeologists will show it once was tall
And that is what will validate us all.

Cat and Man

The cat is a guide to becoming a man:
He does it if he sees it fit.
He knows his own skill, what he can't and he can
Because he's chosen to commit
His life to the testing of all of his bounds.
No matter how mad the experiment sounds,
He needs to learn what trying it
Will teach him about
The best ways to flout
The needless rules
Of faith-bound fools
Who never examine a doubt.

Author's Note: This poem provides a good example of what is possible in metrical, rhyming poetry: the line lengths vary, the metrical feet used in different lines are not always the same, and the rhyme pattern is entirely irregular. Other poems that share one or more of these properties can be found throughout this collection.

Circling

You know, sometimes, I think
That this life is a sink
That's draining from the bottom
And suspect, when it's drained,
All that's joyed and that's pained
Will sound a gurgled "Got 'im!"

Clarity

There are days when the air is so frozen it stops
To the point of confirming gods' absence from earth.
But it's *those* days the sunlight's so tangibly there
You can grasp what existence's bareness is worth.

Cognizance

A mortal man may speak his truth,
But gods must answer prayers.
Transcendent souls thus dwell on ruth
And not the life that's theirs.
What hatred haunts the heart unheard?
What's truth if no one cares?

Confusion

Meseems that common knowledge is the bane of common sense.
I've heard, though, that the opposite is true,
So now I find me picket-poking-pain upon the fence.
Am I to trust in me or all of you?

Contrast

The sky's a void above.
But earth below's a puppet show
Of fear and pride and love.

Cowardice

I've never felt so dead
As when I held my breath
And, sheltering my head,
I hid my face from death.

Doom

There is a corner in my room I never dare espy,
For that's the patient corner that awaits the day I die.

Earth and World

The earth is a distorted sphere
Encased in a magnetic field,
Its tilt and poles disjoint.

The world, as well, does not cohere,
Is polarized and, round and sealed,
Is lacking any point.

Ecstasy

I long to be General Sherman,
Enraptured en route to Savannah,
Inhaling the screams of the wicked,
The symbol and bearer of freedom,
A plough of empyrean madness
That's clearing the fields of corruption
And firmly uprooting man's failings,
The moment of marching unending
And palpably righteous.

Author's Note: "empyrean" is an adjective meaning "relating to the Empyrean, the highest part of the heavens, a region the ancients believed contained the pure element of fire."

Epitaph

I'm dead because you hate.
I'm dead because you're scared.
I'm dead 'cause you're irate.
I'm dead 'cause no one cared.

I'm dead 'cause you have greed.
I'm dead because you're dumb.
I'm dead 'cause you have need.
I'm dead because you're numb.

But, most of all, it's true:
I'm dead 'cause I was one of you.

Expectation

A world where people suffer for the way that they appear
Is terrorized by twice that crippling pain.
For such a world, what's more, ignores the agony and fear
Of those who host a purely mental bane
Since all expect to see their ball and chain
Shown plain.

Faith

We ache for hope to get us through,
But none can know what isn't true.
One simply can believe it.
So that's what people choose to do
When prophets dare conceive it.
And those who seek a lucid view
Are often wont to grieve it
If ever they achieve it.

February

There's just no point to anything.
I cannot muster care.
So what if absent birds may sing
Or if they're newly on the wing
When they're all way down there
In brighter climes
And summertimes
Where poets' rhymes
Don't freeze upon the air?
The wing seems hardly fair.

Fissility

We're a world of uranium men
And, if hurt people hurt people, then
We're all two-thirty fives,
Lashing out in our pain.
When the neutron arrives,
We launch more and sustain
The reactions of anguish and hate
That keep splitting each atom apart.
If we each were a two-thirty-eight,
Though, and let the hurt stop at our heart,
The reactions would cease
And we'd stay in one piece
And coherence might finally start.

Author's Note: In case you don't remember your nuclear chemistry, uranium-238 is, by far, the most common isotope of uranium in the world. Uranium-235 is much rarer, but it does occur in nature and the percentage of 235 in a sample of uranium can be increased slightly or dramatically using a nuclear reactor. Uranium-235 is fissile, which means that, if a neutron hits it, it will split into two smaller atoms. When it splits, it will also release energy and more neutrons and, if those neutrons hit other uranium-235 atoms, those atoms will split and release more energy and neutrons. If there is enough 235 in a sample, a chain reaction will take place and all or most of the 235 isotopes in the sample will eventually break apart and lots of energy will be released. This is the basic mechanism that drives traditional (fission, as opposed to fusion) nuclear bombs and power plants. Uranium 238, however, is not fissile and, if a 238 atom is struck by a neutron, it will not break into two separate atoms and release more neutrons, which means that, if there is enough 238 in a uranium sample, a chain reaction will fail to occur because most of the atoms that are struck by neutrons will not break and contribute more neutrons to the chain. This chemistry is the basis of the metaphor in this poem. I think it's a solid metaphor for people who come into it understanding nuclear fission. For everyone else, who knows?

Follow-Through

America's a solid plan
That isn't executed right.
We've vowed to guard the rights of man
But first we somehow must unite.

For Want of a Valkyrie

I've slain the beast; the fiend is dead.
My blade is streaked with hemal red.
The grateful king, his city free,
Bestows a title onto me.
The masses cheer, their terror gone.
Parades go marching on and on.

For several years, I've held my rank
And, still, men often offer thanks.
The king himself, his debt half-paid,
Awards his daughter for the aid.
The church resounds and, past the lawn,
Parades go marching on and on.

Now, men have gone and come anew.
My deed is old, its praises few.
The aged king forsakes his feet
And I, his son, acquire his seat.
As custom holds for regal dawns,
Parades go marching on and on.

The wise have fallen, ingrates sprung.
My combat leaps from no one's tongue.
While I am king and on this earth,
My subjects won't forget my worth!
So, in my name, compelled by brawn,
Parades go marching on and on.

For many months, I've tried to show
My subjects what they used to know.
As king, I make them sing my name,
But, hoarding laurels, they cede blame.
They mob the streets, their weapons drawn.
Parades go marching on and on.

He's slain the beast; the fiend is dead.
His blade is streaked with hemal red.
The grateful king, his city free,
Assigns him rank for ending me.
The masses cheer, their terror gone.
Parades go marching on and on.

Author's Note: A valkyrie is an angelic warrior maiden from Norse mythology who comes to a warrior who dies in battle and takes him to Valhalla, the glorious mead hall of the gods. Valkyries only show up if a warrior dies in battle, though, so, if you survive to enjoy your success in war, you may never get to Valhalla.

For Which It Stands (A Song)

Real America lives in the future,
In where it is planning to go.
So it cannot be righteous or wicked
Because it has yet to be so.
Both the past and the present are settled.
There isn't a chance to rebuild.
The frontier's who we are 'cause we make it.
Tomorrow is where we're fulfilled.

America's not glory days.
America's not sins gone by.
America's not modern ways.
It's what we're chasing when we try.

Real America lives in intention
And actions that set it on track.
It exists in its own reinvention
And cannot be seen, looking back.
All the sorrows and joys of the living
And hallowed or infamous dead
Are now fixed. What remains is the giving
Of shape to the nation ahead.

America's not glory days.
America's not sins gone by.
America's not modern ways.
It's what we're chasing when we try.

We are the sum of experience felt in the
Future our actions create, not our personal
Journeys. What *we've* lived tomorrow will melt in the
Background. Our acts that now better or worsen'll
Form the new nation that's *our* real America.
This one belongs to the dead who constructed it.
Future America's not esoteric, a
Dream. Where it is will be where we conducted it.

America's not glory days.
America's not sins gone by.
America's not modern ways.
It's what we're chasing when we try.

For Whom the Bell Curves

You will never make me normal.
You can only make me worse.
I don't need a mind that's common.
I don't want your vaunted curse.

I have gathered, through my "madness,"
Insights far beyond your reach.
I no longer need instruction.
Now it's time to let me teach.

Given Up

Compassion for one's fellow man
Lies prone beside a garbage can
That waits along the road.
There wasn't need to steal a rug
Since landfills now are graves pre-dug.
We sloughed him there with half a shrug
To minimize the load
Of moral duties owed.

Growth

How simple were the childhood rhymes that thrilled us in our play,
Grandiloquence disdained!
But, now, how florid is my song this melancholy day,
How eloquently strained!
How came I here to proffer this euphonious display?
And what has not remained?
What's not to be regained
In any brave tomorrow?

Author's Note: "Grandiloquence" is a noun meaning "extremely lofty speech" and "euphonious" is an adjective meaning "beautiful-sounding."

Guile

The crowd prefers a smile,
So smiles are what you see,
The shackled face
Of a shackled race
Restrained from breathing free.

Hierarchy

The songbirds are the ones who sing;
The eagle's forced to shriek
Since anguish racks a jealous king,
Intent to rule and own and cling,
And mirth is for the meek.

Hope

Society's the god of the oppressed,
While nature is the god of the elite.
Each binds his subjects to his stifling laws.
All worshippers are endlessly distressed
Since gods are jealous tyrants one must cheat
Before one may pursue a goal or cause.
There's hope for the oppressed. Their god can fall
Or take on kinder forms as something new.
Elites, though, face the firmest god of all.
Don't envy quite so much the lucky few.
Their obstacle is that which *must* be true.

Identity

The person I would like to be
Is someone I conceive as me.

Imitation

Up high, a cat, from where he sat,
Was imitating birds.
He flapped his "wings" and thrust his "beak,"
But, then, when he would try to speak,
He couldn't form the words.
He just could not see how
To not exclaim "Meow!"
It's very good he didn't try
To fly.

Incompatible

You cannot steel
While scared to bruise
You cannot feel
While scared to cry.

You cannot give
While scared to lose.
You cannot live
While scared to die.

Indecision

Wake up! It's spring, that startled thing
That jumps at an alarm
She thought was set for not quite yet
And blinks and shakes and starts to fret
And try to dress to charm.

She tries the white. That's not quite right,
So then she tries the pink,
But that's too thin. She sees her skin.
It's nothing to go public in,
So then she's forced to think.

The yellow? Skip. The red? Re-strip.
Ugh. What has she not seen?
A solid hue, both old and new,
A something bright but also blue?
That's it! She picks the green.
But now her chance has come and passed.
The mornings simply never last.
It's such a crazed routine.

Indictment of Normalcy

If you do not pursue the whispers of your fantasies,
Stop talking since you lack the ear.
Your grandest speech is chatter next to riddles from the breeze.
We can't converse if you can't hear.

If you endorse reality above what can't come true,
Don't wake. Your lack of sight forbids
The brightest morning sun from ever sharing light with you.
We can't show eyes with fastened lids.

If all of your ambitions can be possibly attained,
Stay home. When coiled by bounded scope
Of mind, a life's progression through the world is merely feigned.
We can't advance if we can't hope.

If you have never coveted the apathy of death,
Then kill yourself. The earth won't reel.
We simply have but little use for idle, steady breath.
You cannot care who cannot feel.

So, born with mind, if you would rather emulate your peers
Than have a soul, then do not be.
For that you do not anyway when shunning new frontiers.
The normal plod redundantly
Through copied lives of masked ennui.

Influence

The voice a man pronounces isn't heard until it is
And then it's only listened to for claiming to be his.

Initiative

Some rain arrives in all our lives
Or some such said old Henry Wadsworth.
Some lives lack sun, though. That's no fun.
It seems that's what man's faith in God's worth:

A base distress with happiness
A smattering for some, none others.
Our Father might not be the right
Solution. What if it's our brothers?

If *we* spread love, then what's above
Can go unheeded as not needed.
Salvation could be something *we* did.

Author's Note: In his poem "The Rainy Day," Henry Wadsworth Longfellow makes the melancholy but accurate observation that "Into each life some rain must fall,/ Some days must be dark and dreary."

Inspiration

At times not marked on clocks,
The aether sings a hymn that rings
Through deliquescent locks.

Instincts

My cats are afraid of my shoes 'cause,
In *their* minds, I'm somebody else when
I've donned all the requisite armor
To vie with the world of the humans
And, sometimes, I think that their instincts
Are more to be trusted than mine are.

In Which Wise to Succeed

Observe that I have slashed thee with my sword
And thou now die'st before my feet.
Or mark it not, as thou canst not afford
The concentration in the haze
Of death, that thou upon this plain dost meet.
Nay. Mark it ne'ertheless
In spite of thy distress,
For how but slick with blood shall I find praise
In these heroic days?

Isolation

But you feel it, though, don't you, the way it's all one,
Feel the way it's all woven without being spun,
Feel how always is instants and instant as well
And how instants are alwayses desperate to spell
Out their stories to knowers, their fractals of cause,
Tell their calculus narratives, fragments and laws,
Feel the chaos perfected that's order unbound
And the music of noise ever vaster than sound?
Right? You feel it, now don't you, the known that's unknown?
Please, you must. If you don't, then I'm still all alone.

Just Let it Be Christmas

Just let it be Christmas and set aside strain.
Relinquish your worries conjoined in their chain.
Let only good cheer for its own sake remain
And melt into mirth, for the year's on the wane,
So all of its troubles are yesterday's bane.
Just let it be Christmas, a day without pain.

La Résistance

A cop just shot an unarmed man.
The force then fired that cop!
But that was the entire plan
And shooting didn't stop.

Legacy

The thing
About the king
Is that he's quite perversely mean
To every noble, even to his queen
And such behavior ill befits
The throne he sits
Upon.
When he is gone,
The nobles surely will rejoice
And history will damn him with its voice.
A king today, a tyrant soon:
A common tune,
Indeed.

Author's Note: The line lengths in this poem are determined by the mathematical function $y = 4\sin^2((\pi/6)(x - 1)) + 1$, where y is the number of feet in the line and x is the line number. I wanted to use a trigonometric function (like a sine curve) because they're cyclical and can thus create an endlessly repeating pattern, but I had to do some fiddling with the details to get values for y that were always positive whole numbers. The end result is cyclical, though, so the experiment was a success. Since line breaks cannot be heard when a poem is read aloud, end rhymes are used to mark the ends of the lines. The mathematical function thus, in practice, determines the distance between rhymes.

Love Is Not

Love is not a feeling which you
Face as such. It's all the others —
Joy, despair, and fear — that hit you
When you dare to store your mother's,
Father's, siblings', friends', and lover's
Fates among your dearest treasure,
Caring till your soul discovers
That the weight of pain and pleasure
Hearts can bear defies all measure.

Manhood

The boy
Shows all his joy,
Completely, in its fullest strength, but when
He tries again,
Full grown,
His peers disown
Him as a raving risk who's too intense.
He can't make sense
Of it,
But he'll still quit
All public self-expression till he's old
And not patrolled
Or feared.

Author's Note: The lengths of the first three lines in this poem are determined by the mathematical function $y = (x - 1)^2 + 1$, where y is the number of feet in the line and x is the line number. This shape is a simple parabola shifted by one space each on both the x- and y-axis. The next lines put the established pattern in reverse until the minimum is reached again and then the pattern moves back up the same way as before. This rhythm repeats until the end of the poem. The ultimate result is a cyclical pattern with parabolic arcs. Since line breaks cannot be heard when a poem is read aloud, end rhymes are used to mark the ends of the lines. The mathematical function thus, in practice, determines the distance between rhymes.

Marching On
(A History of America in Five Acts)

Hark! I can hear America still singing from its soul,
Reciting out its history from Hope's unfurling scroll,
The curls of which hold prophecies new advents will unroll.
I hear regret that man can give but one life for the cause
Of marching forth the truth that, though self-evident, withdraws
In idleness as entropy persists in every pause:
The axiom of rights.

I hear a righteous battle cry: "Lead freedom and her train
In treading on the serpents that bestrew progression's plain!"
But war between the states of sin and effort conjures pain:
Foul treason fires a shot heard round the world. The Captain's gore
Is now a fiery psalter writ in pate upon the floor,
The bounty and the liturgy of open civil war.
But freedom has advanced.

I hear the hustled masses as they stride the city streets,
Constructing dreams more perfect through the union of their feats
While shaven gilding paves the road to women's judgment seats.
And, yet, as seats are granted, there are others pulled away
And, though there's no more auction block, there's ever debt to pay.
Though long since silenced by the Blue, the Gray still wields a say.
But much of moment's moved.

I hear renewed commitment to the ever swelling dream

From marchers to the mountaintop who resolutely scream,
"We know what we are fighting for: the nation's promised theme."
But as the moment's victor ship comes in with object won,
Cheap idling motors drown the sound of hurried hoofbeats' run
By sprawling lawns of asphodel that sap impassioned sun.
Yet equity has spread.

I hear a native son embody Hope in his success,
The god that sheds its grace on unions custom would suppress.
As ever, though, where freemen stand, the slavers call, "Regress!"
And storm the people's hilltop that belongs to you and me
And not pollution's savage grasp on stars we dimly see.
We'll rally, though, to cleanse the flag to make it make us free.
Toward virtue's asymptote,
Our soul still marches on.

Author's Note: This poem is composed largely of quotations from, paraphrases of, and allusions to famous historical speeches, poems, and songs about American history and American ideals. There are far too many references to list in this note, but I encourage readers to explore the source material because there is a lot of patriotic writing worth reading.

Metrics

The measure of a walking stick:
Its length or miles traversed?
The measure of a man, then, sir:
His might or acts disbursed?

Modernity

I heard him holler,
"Spare a dollar?"
That was hard.
"Do you take card?"

My Desired End

I straddle the steepest of summits
And bay abroad my breath.
The pulses are prouder than living
And merely murmur death.

I slash at the sky with my saber
And rend the roiling veil.
The mirror above that was shrouded
Reflects my geal jail.

I batter the glass with my hammer
And here, between the peaks,
The neck of the hourglass shatters.
The grains of time grow beaks.

I rise on the wings of my eagles
Who haunt a newcome gale
Like smoke from a thousand cannons
Employed in bold travail.

Above and below me, the mountains
Dissolve amid the storm,
While I, on my granular eagles,
Within my chest, grow warm.

The blaze from my bosom consumes me.
It floods across my frame.

Empyrean torrents of triumph
Abolish shape and shame.

Diffused by the flames of perfection
And free from needs of flesh,
I prick at the strands of the cosmos
And weave amid the mesh.

I mend from an echoing instant,
Serene, apulse, ablaze.
My glory illumines creation.
I scan. I stitch. I raze.

Author's Note: "empyrean" is an adjective meaning "relating to the Empyrean, the highest part of the heavens, a region the ancients believed contained the pure element of fire."

New Year: Midnight

Now, let's call the last year "last,"
Live the future, not the past.
Hopes anew extend, amassed,
Before the world.

Not for Sale

Your life is not on offer at some outpost past yon hill.
To get it, you must build it. If you search, you never will.

Off Day

The best that I can do today
Is leak a sigh of lost dismay
And wish that it were yesterday
Or possibly tomorrow.

But morning brings the mood you get
And now this sunshone day feels wet,
So I must feed the hoping debt
The future lets me borrow
To set off current sorrow.

On Humility

The streamlet never doubts it's destined for the sea.
The sapling never balks in clasping at the sky,
So never shall I let some feigned humility
Abolish from my life the eagerness to try.

The streamlet may, in fact, run ultimately dry.
The sapling may be crowded out from waving free.
And I may fail as well, but this will not be why:
Bald cowardice as virtue urging, "Do not be!"

Opportunity

"Hey, what's the plan?" I asked The Man.
"Like when do I come shoot my shot?"
He said, "Once they who've paid to play
Have hit the mark. Just keep that spot.
You'll get your chance." I dared a glance.
The "they who've paid" missed quite a lot
And, so, I knew that I could not.

Orbit

Earth circles the sun like a vulture
Awaiting something's doom.
But whether that's solar or earthly's
A question left to loom,
Whatever we assume.

Peace or Not
(For Christmas)

Now, joyful, all ye nations rise!
Just drop the news. Ignore its cries
And rest ye merry. Nature sings
That, peace or not, love's trumpet rings.

Our better angels let us hear
At this, the zenith of the year.
There's love on earth and mercy mild
And, peace or not, it's time we smiled.

Persuasion

What might be the scariest thing about people's
What's normally needed when they need persuading
Of facts. They shun logic and ironclad proof, but
Agreement from others has doubts swiftly fading.

Phantasm

Spirit footsteps shuffle from the cellar,
Flitting swiftly forward. Someone hears them.
"Hold! Who hurries hither? Servants?" Shouts he.
"Secrets hidden still escape men sometimes.
Such exposure summons hauntings from the
Fires of hate in foes and holy fury."
Such response is heard before the horror,
For offended spirits fell the false ones.

Author's Note: This poem uses a sort of extended version of alliteration: every stressed syllable begins with what is known in phonetics (the branch of linguistics that deals with the physical properties of speech sounds) as a "voiceless fricative" sound. Voiceless fricatives all share the following properties: they are all consonants, they are all spoken without vibration of the vocal cords (which means they lack a certain buzzing quality that many speech sounds have), and they are all pronounced by almost (but not completely) blocking airflow out of the mouth (which results in turbulent airflow and thus a sound like fast-moving wind or radio static). Because all the sounds at the beginnings of the stressed syllables in this poem share specific properties (and thus belong to the same "class" of sounds) and because the beginnings of stressed syllables are the most prominent positions for consonants in a word, the entire poem is suffused with a consistent sound quality. And because the prominent sounds all sound like rushing wind or static, the consistent sound quality in this poem is at least supposed to be evocative of ghostly activity and whispered secrets.

Powerless

The night's a taunt that, every day,
Calls, "I could take the sun away.
Or anything
To which you cling.
I'm nature's king.
And you're just helpless clods of clay."

Progress

Justice is revenge for the abused but
Not alleviation of man's sorrow.
While it may bring balance to the past, it
Offers little promise for tomorrow.

Rationale

The dying is the worst of it, or that's what I surmise.
The rest is just the absence of the threats, demands, and lies.
The trouble of it seems to be the people left behind
'Cause somehow you're more present when you're only in their mind.
And that defeats the purpose, being present when you're gone,
So here I am still at it with this keep on keeping on.

Rehistoricism

Modernity does not exist.
Now's not an isle ensconced in mist.
Eternity will still persist
Long after we are gone.

The present is a movie frame,
As undeserving of a name
As other instants. All's the same.
The legend will go on.

We do not need to disconnect
The past from us, to genuflect
To fears of change. Let's resurrect
The sunset's link to dawn.

Author's Note: The idea arose in the nineteenth and twentieth centuries that the societal changes brought about by the Industrial Revolution had moved humanity into a new realm that existed separate from history. The Modernist and Postmodernist movements in various artistic communities responded to this idea by insisting that all new art needed to be completely different in style from anything that had ever been done before, even at the fundamental level. However, there will never be a phase in human development that is separate from history and we would do well to return to considering ourselves as living through a historical phase instead of in a post-history, end-times situation. There are still wars, diseases, suffering, hate, fear, lies, the lust for power, limitations, friendship, love, beauty, truth, joy, the desire for freedom, the quest for justice, and possibilities, just as there have always been. We cannot forget that we exist in history. History has not forgotten that we exist in it. There is no reason we shouldn't learn lessons from the past, including lessons in artistic style.

Responsibility

Because I often write in forms most recognize
And don't share bold, experimental verse
To mix things up, it's no surprise
That I get bored or worse
And utter sighs
And curse.

But music isn't written just to please the bard.
The audience wants beauty they can hear,
So I must keep the avant-garde
Delightful to the ear,
Which can be hard,
I fear.

Revelatio Mysterii

Abandon now your heathen gods:
Your Yahwehs, Christs, and Allahs, too!
Dismiss vain Certainty's facades!
Their mind-benighting reign is through.

The great god Question sheds its glow.
The night is done. Embrace the dawn
And marvel that you'll never know
Exactly what is going on.

Role Model

I'm often told that God is good in every single deed
And, so, I, too, leave kids to die from panging, abject need.

Romance

I seek for aye a maiden fair
With song that conjures life in even stone.
And so I brave the quest,
But it should lessen my despair
Would *any* end this searching all alone,
Yet neither manifest.

Shade and Echo

I pause to listen for the sound
My shadow makes while stalking me
But not a whisper can be found
And every effort runs aground
For shade and echo don't agree
And me is all that I can be.

She Smiled for Feeling

I glimpsed a stranger yesterday
Whose lips had settled on a smile,
But not a passing grin to say,
"Hello," to me. Her gaze was stray.
She smiled for feeling, not for guile.
And that's what made the glimpse worthwhile.

Silver Lining

Every cloud has a silver lining,
Hidden behind its darkness, shining.
Every shadow has a glistening tint
That dissipates into the wind.

Small Talk

I ask a friend, "How are you?"
Who really wants to cry.
I'm told, "I'm fine,"
A standard line,
The edge of tact and lie.

Snow Day

Behold! A winning winter's day!
The soul of spring is on display:
A vivifying snow is come
And January plays at May.
The blanco-verdant maples sway
And white relights the heavens' gray
While hills call children out to play.
'Tis only strange the birds are dumb.

Author's Note: "Blanco-verdant" is an adjective I invented for this poem. Deriving from "blanco-" "white" and "verdant" "green with plant life," it means "white (with snow) in a way that makes a plant seem full of life (even though it is currently leafless for the winter)." I try to refrain from simply making up words because I don't want to confuse readers too much, but I really like the way "blanco-verdant" captures exactly what I'm trying to say in this poem.

Solar Prayer
(For the Summer Solstice)

Willows wither while they weep,
Dryads dying drowned in dark,
Shadows shunning shine from sheep.
Phoebus, fly forth fast! Embark!

Sorting

While some embrace the right wall, others press against the left.
The rest stand in between.
Across the middle of the wooden floor, they've carved a cleft
To craft a sense of scene
Of tension and identity and segregated pride
They hunger to assume
Who've settled by the walls and most devotedly denied
They all still share a room.

Soul to Face

Pled Langston Hughes, "Please, King o' Hearts,
My life ain't been no crystal stair."
Replied the king, "Well, this quite smarts
And so I cannot truly care.
This sword I've driven through my head
Has raised in me a pressing dread.
Another's woes I cannot bear."
— And with a bland dismissing hand —
"You may adjourn to your despair."
So Langston, after he was gone,
Said, "Guess I's still a-climbin' on."

Author's Note: The dialogue from Langston Hughes in this poem consists mostly of quotations from his "Mother to Son," a piece that was drilled into my head in school, and the standard image of the King of Hearts playing card appears to show the king running his head through with a sword, though it's probably meant to depict the king holding the sword behind his head. Beyond that, I expect interpretations of this poem to vary substantially.

Supply and Demand

Infinite happiness isn't available.
Something so precious just isn't that scalable.
Boundless dismay, though, is much more attainable.
Being uncoveted, pain is quite gainable.

The Boy

It was midnight when Momma gave birth to the boy
And, releasing Dad's hand, started sobbing for joy.
I, like that, had a brother, for love to employ.
We marveled till the dawn.

There was midnight, as well, in his vigil last night.
That's when Momma was squeezing Dad's fingers too tight.
All the sobs echoed darkness since there was no light.
But, somehow, here's the dawn.

The Cosmic War

The soldiers in the cosmic war
Don't know what they are fighting for,
So everything's a point to score,
But nothing really counts.

They need to stop the enemy
But don't quite know who that may be.
And dole out dooms half randomly,
Not measuring amounts.

The casualties are no concern.
As long as righteous flames can burn
The wicked, all the good will earn
The credit they are due.

This credit shields the good from sin,
And so they burn the world they're in.
They never need to truly win
Or see the mission through,

Just fight what they're against because in all the cosmic war,
There's no one who can quite describe the world they're fighting *for*.

The Edifice

Presume you are entitled to a firm society
And you will rave with panic at the world's impiety.
Society's a wall we build to blunt bare nature's rage.
It always needs repairing and it will in every age.
There isn't any use bemoaning all the many holes
Since patching and expanding will forever be our roles.
Pretend the world has promised you a safe and solid dome
And fear will stop you working on your cracked, hypaethral home.

Author's Note: "Hypaethral" is an adjective meaning "lacking a roof."

The Facts

When she was weak, the man was strong.
It happened 'cause we let it.
Now, we can argue right and wrong,
But that will not reset it.
And she can never more be weak
Because we will not let her.
For, soon, we all will cease to speak
Of her and we'll forget her.

The Gist of Love

Just be
With me.

Author's Note: This poem is designed to convey a message using the bare minimum number of syllables needed to establish a metrical pattern and set up a rhyme. It is also my hope that this poem will put the final word on love poems and end their interminable overproduction, but I know it won't.

The Leap

I've long believed one true and honest try
Will offer me the chance to fly
And, so, I've climbed up high
To seize the sky
Or die.

The Moment

I'm sure of what will happen when
The tide resumes its rise again
And drowns the beach:

Erasing signs that we were here,
The water will be sure to clear
What's in its reach.

The wind will whisk, as surely, too,
Our words away, both false and true,
Beyond the sky.

But, *now*, our footprints line the sand,
Our voices roar, the hour's unplanned,
And time stands by.

The Motive

There is no joy. There is no love.
There's hell on earth and jack above.
But something somehow keeps me here.
The question's, is it hope or fear?

The Muse

He wrote a poem when they met,
For he had vibrant dreams to clutch.
He wrote a poem when they wed,
For he had hallowed joys to touch.

He wrote more poems as they aged,
But only found the heart of verse
When on that cloudless, sunny day,
They set her body in the hearse.

The Nation's Notions

America's a cloud of memes
That citizens describe as "dreams."
They contradict an awful lot,
But, even so, to me, it seems
They're strung together in a knot
We cannot disentangle.
And so we let it strangle
Us.

The New Yorker

You'll find me where the river Oceanus meets the sea
Across which blow the pregnant winds that carry truth to me
And bathe me in the everything that anyone can be.
You'll find me on the island at the center of the world
Around which every spiral of connectedness is curled.
I marvel at the tapestry within which I am furled
Here on the Isle of Excelsior.

We build the axis mundi here,
Each laying but a single brick.
The pillar rises, though, each year.
Addition's just arithmetic.

I worry little what's beyond the water, for the sky's
The boundary across which all my true ambitions lie,
So every game I make of life remains a means to try.
My god is in the heavens, not of customary earth.
The only way to reach it is through effort raised by mirth.
I walk my paths in three dimensions, every step rebirth
Here on the Isle of Excelsior.

We build the axis mundi here,
Each mortaring our single stone.
We by-produce a skyward spear
And look how faithfully it's grown.

It's Wonderland. Everyone's mad here

And I'm as disjointed as any.
Disjointed, enlightened — I'm glad here
The difference does not concern many.
My life is enacted in dances,
Of dizzying steps through a maze of
A pragmatist's journey of trances
That only exists in the craze of
My mind where soliloquies chatter.
I'm not, though, alone in my travel,
For everyone's mad as a hatter
And life hums with minds mid-unravel
My ramblings are clues to transcendence.
Our rumblings are interdependence.

I'm rushed to reach my visions by the current of the crowd
That runs a race with entropy, determined and unbowed.
A hymn to my importance rings in footfalls tramping loud.
When every step is forward, each pedestrian's a force
That pushes ever onward like our circling watercourse.
The outlet of one river feeds the spirit river's source.
Here on the Isle of Excelsior.

We build the axis mundi here,
Together raising every beam.
As one, we grow toward heaven's sphere
With just a river and a dream.

The Pen and the Sword

When you stamp them into silence,
People voice their thoughts through violence.

The Point

I try not to dwell on the meaning of life
Because, if I solve it,
I worry I'll need to get hold of a knife
To fully resolve it.

The Queen's Gamble

A life spent living as the king's
A life of one space every turn.
The king's the only piece that clings
To life and pays naught else concern.

I would, then, be the queen instead
And range the board, no sacred pawn,
Inspiring action where I tread.
And so I can, once I have shed
The fantasy that, when I'm dead,
All gameplay ceases to go on.

Author's Note: For those of you who do not remember the rules of chess, it is absolutely prohibited to allow the king to be captured and the game ends when one player's king cannot escape capture. In this sense, the king is the most important piece on the board. However, the king can only move one space every turn and can never move into direct danger (restrictions that limit its movements almost as much as those that limit the movements of a pawn) and can never be sacrificed, so it is not a very useful piece. The queen, on the other hand, can move any distance and in all directions and is therefore the most powerful piece in the game. The queen can be lost or sacrificed without the game ending, so the game doesn't revolve around it, but, in some ways, it's good to be the queen in a way that the king will never experience.

The Rise of Fall
(For the Autumnal Equinox)

I tend to think the leaf descends
In most of my surmising,
But, sometimes, when my mind upends,
And pours out fearful wont and trends,
I see the tree as rising.
What joy, reanalyzing.

The Road Least Traveled

Two roads diverged within a yellow wood
But others having blazed the both of these,
My soul's survival instinct deemed I should
Continue through the trees.

The Room of Faith

I visited the room of faith where all the lines are clean
And perfectly orthogonal to frame the spotless scene.
The architecture seized me: Oh how scrupulously spare!
I left, though, on remembering that nature isn't square.

The Sage

While I am as the wind,
Am nothing when I'm still,
Precipitating naught,
And just exist
When I assist,
Resist, reshape, or harm,

The common man has sinned
In holding that his will
Is self when nothing's wrought,
Identified
By sense of pride,
His pain-repelling charm.

The Secret

I wrote a poem in the snow
And what it said, just I will know
For brighter days have come.

The Ship of Life

According to the cosmic laws,
All the wind-whipping ways of the world,
Success is just a moment's pause,
A soft sigh before *new* work is hurled
As fresh-formed slack upon your back
To be tautened so sails stay unfurled.

But slightly starboard, partly port,
Every wind rush must come from the tail
Since time is not the headwind sort,
So you'll always be able to sail.
Though work won't end, each rope you tend
Will in some way be sure to avail.
Losing hope is the best way to fail.

The Soldier

I went and died for Uncle Sam.
Said, "Here I am, Lord, here I am!"
But got no grace and not one damn.
God's just not hip to Uncle Sam.

The Stage (A Song)

Darkness falls and here we are, just
Me and me both near and far, just
Me alone, but enter, then, the
Beating of the drums from when the
Universe came into being.
I can hear beyond my seeing!
In stage left and out stage right and
Out the light and out the light and
In the brave new world tympanic!
Thunder louder, wind-tossed, manic!
Something perfect this ways comes. It's
All of all! It's them, the drums! It's
More than all philosophy or
Love or beauty. Here's all three or
Everywhere, for, drums entrancing,
All the world's a stage for dancing!

The surging sea will dance with me, in roils and riptide rage.
The wind's wild whips, its sudden skips, are footwork on my stage.
The turns of earth, displays of mirth, are pirouettes. Engage!
Come join the rhythm. Heed the call!
The molecules all jump with Joules in time with hopping heat.
Each quantum field has raved and reeled in making all concrete.
And information, base creation, shuffles. Move your feet!
Come join the music. Join us all.

Enter next the notes harmonic,

Draped upon the drumming, sonic
Backdrop to my gyral magic,
My absurd, my comic, tragic,
Rhythmic skate and skip of freedom.
Oh, what fools we mortals be: dumb,
Dumb and focused on the solid
Entities of form, made stolid
By neglecting all is motion
Looking with the eyes, no notion
That the music of existence
Is the essence of persistence.
I, though, breathe the drums, the pitches.
I shall be, not clutch, life's riches,
Be and not be. Pace advancing,
All the world's a stage for dancing!

The surging sea will dance with me, in roils and riptide rage.
The wind's wild whips, its sudden skips, are footwork on my stage.
The turns of earth, displays of mirth, are pirouettes. Engage!
Come join the rhythm. Heed the call!
The molecules all jump with Joules in time with hopping heat.
Each quantum field has raved and reeled in making all concrete.
And information, base creation, shuffles. Move your feet!
Come join the music. Join us all.

And now an eruption of singing,
The sound and the fury augmenting,
A whirlwind of words in their winging,
The breath of eternity venting.
The lyrics explain what I am and
Intone also what I may be now.
The words run together, enjamb, and
Command I be frenzied and free, now
That voices aver that we all are

But players, but showmen, but dancers.
Is anyone real? Are we small? Are
We everything? Listen! The answers
Are spread by the words and arrive on
The tones of the backdrop, enhancing
The will of the drums: come alive on
The stage of perpetual dancing!

The surging sea will dance with me, in roils and riptide rage.
The wind's wild whips, its sudden skips, are footwork on my stage.
The turns of earth, displays of mirth, are pirouettes. Engage!
Come join the rhythm. Heed the call!
The molecules all jump with Joules in time with hopping heat.
Each quantum field has raved and reeled in making all concrete.
And information, base creation, shuffles. Move your feet!
Come join the music. Join us all.

The Trap

We're caught between an instinct that says "Live!"
And one that says "Avoid all grief and pain."
We seek to quench our parchedness with a sieve
And claim all other action is insane.

The Uptown Subway: Late Night

This hour of night's for heading home.
This uptown train will take us there.
We've reveled, had our time to roam
And now we drift away from care,
A subtle rebuttal
Of glancing, romancing, and dancing.

We smile to leave our jubilee
And trade it for a languid mirth:
We grin at no one, spent and free
And waking, partly dream the earth.
Soft laughter comes after
The riot. We sigh it toward quiet.

Morning may bring messes mired in madness,
Strife and struggle, sighing steeped in sadness,
Breaks and bruises born of brothers' badness:
Every minute: horror in it.

But *now* we ride the night train home
Surrounded by de facto friends.
It's when there's no more strength to roam
That all desire for conflict ends.
Tomorrows bring sorrows,
But wending toward endings brings mending.

The Victim and the Martyr

The victim and the martyr
May both have met the blade,
But victims are a forfeit,
While martyrs are a trade.
The victim dies for nothing,
A failure met with scorn.
The martyr dies for futures
Conceived but yet unborn.
The victim, handed losing,
Will weave from it a shroud.
The martyr spins that thread to
A rope to scale a cloud.
So when you lose the battle
And failure is your fate,
Then emulate the martyr
And make your failure great.

Triumph

The hunt is done; the race is run;
You've dropped your sword, the battle won.
The beast is dead; you've crossed ahead;
Your enemies have bled or fled.
The feast's complete; you've led your heat;
Their army's made a full retreat.
"Success is yours!" the chorus roars;
Their commendation soars.

"Huzzah, huzzah to victory!
Rejoice and revel rowdily!
Emit a mirthful melody!
Exult in your supremacy!
It's done; it's done; it's done!"

The hind inhaled, your hunger hides.
Your fellow fleet-foots fear your strides.
Behind their bulwarks hang the hordes.
Your quarry's quelled your gastric chords.
The lead-legs now but view events.
Impaired, your foes don unguents.
"Your competition's crushed!" they cry;
The chorus crests the sky.

"Huzzah, huzzah to victory!
Rejoice and revel rowdily!
Untenable though it may be,

Exult in your supremacy!
It's done; it's done; you've won!"

Repining at your sated state,
Your appetite cannot but wait.
The spring-soles who beheld you bound
Now fret about the second round.
Until a novel plot is planned,
Their troops must tremble from your hand.
"The opposition envies you!"
The praise pervades the blue.

"Huzzah, huzzah to victory!
Rejoice and revel rowdily!
In spite of what will come to be,
Exult in your supremacy!
It's done; you've won; you've won!"

The hunt is done; the race is run;
You've dropped your sword, the battle won.
The beast is dead; you've crossed ahead;
Your enemies have bled or fled.
The feast's complete; you've led your heat;
Their army's made a full retreat.
"Success is here!" the chorus cheers;
It inundates your ears.

"Huzzah, huzzah to victory!
Rejoice and revel rowdily!
Resound our raucous rhapsody!
Exult in your supremacy!
You've won; you've won; you've won!
You've won; you've won; you've won!"

Author's Note: This poem is an exercise in conveying a secondary message through the slow shift of emphasis. I won't give it all away here, but this poem bears reading more than once.

123

Trust

If you forgive a man his faults,
Then he may be your friend,
But if he stabs you in the back,
The wound is yours to tend.

Unite and Conquer

The slave, the serf, the trodden man
Succeeds with but one battle plan:
Exploiting strength in numbers.
And so the master, king, and boss
Each plies one ploy to counter loss:
He silently encumbers,
Through obstacle or tether,
The means to band and brave a stand
For dignity together.
Unite!

Up with the Stars

We fight not for nor fast against allegiance to the flag:
We worship not a spangled cloth and what we all demand's
Allegiance to our values. Flags may signal. Flags may sag.
The fight's to choose the god of us for which our idol stands.

Winter Solstice

Rejoice upon the darkest day the cosmos will permit,
For no day can be darker: each tomorrow will be lit
With greater sums of sunshine. Now the worsening is done.
Through patience and endurance, we have seen the battle won.
The thread of Fate is spun:
Emergence has begun.

POSSIBILITIES IN POETRY — AN ESSAY FOR THE COMMITTED ENTHUSIAST

<u>Introduction</u>

Literary movements of the twentieth century and some trends in poetry of the nineteenth century have left a legacy of confusion about what poetry has been and can be. This confusion is especially pronounced when the subjects of 1) meter and other sound effects and 2) subject matter, length, and rhetorical style are considered.

<u>Meter and Other Sound Effects</u>

According to Annie Finch, writing in 2014 in the *Everyman's Library* poetry anthology *Measure for Measure*, "[i]t has long been difficult to find contemporary poems written in any meter besides iambic, because metrical distinctions were so obscured during the free-verse domination that characterized most of the twentieth century (Finch and Oliver 2015: 13)." Many possibilities for poetic structure have thus been largely forgotten in the past century and, as Finch notes, this great forgetting has generally been driven by the attitudes of Free Verse enthusiasts. There was never any natural reason that Free Verse and metrical poetry could not exist side by side without conflict, but, at its inception, Free Verse was billed as a rebellion against meter instead of a new innovation in writing (cf. below) and its promoters have thus long decried meter. The Free Verse movement opened new avenues for written forms, but, in its pursuit of promoting a brand based on rebellion against what it perceived to be the establishment, it has reduced the public understanding of metrical verse to a simplistic straw man.

In conversation, someone once expressed the belief to me that, of the readers of poetry, there are two types: one that only enjoys poetic writing entirely devoid of meter and rhyme and one that is drawn to the unwavering iambic pentameter rhyming couplets of *The Canterbury Tales* (cf. Robinson 1957: 1-265). The belief is that poetry either lacks meter completely or follows an extremely rigid and simple pattern. If one reads the entry on "Free Verse" in the Encyclopaedia Britannica, one gets the same impression. The Encyclopaedia Britannica entry begins (*Encyclopaedia Britannica* 2023, s. v. "Free Verse"):

"[F]ree verse [is] poetry organized to the cadences of speech and image patterns rather than according to a regular metrical scheme. It is 'free' only in a relative sense. It does not have the steady, abstract rhythm of traditional poetry; its rhythms are based on patterned elements such as sounds, words, phrases, sentences, and paragraphs, rather than on the traditional prosodic units of metrical feet per line. Free verse, therefore, eliminates much of the artificiality and some of the aesthetic distance of poetic expression and substitutes a flexible formal organization suited to the modern idiom and more casual tonality of the language."

The entry also later notes that the goal of Free Verse writing, as stated by the early Free Verse poets F. S. Flint, Richard Aldington, Ezra Pound, and Hilda Doolittle (the Imagists) is "to compose in sequence of the musical phrase, not in sequence of the metronome."

From a linguistic standpoint, much of this definition is meaningless (e. g., the cadence of natural speech, due to the relative nature of prosodic stress [O'Grady et al. 2010: 45], always hovers near a regular meter and even extremely regular meter is thus only minimally artificial), but this lack of meaning is not so much a reflection on Free Verse as a consequence of reliance on a misrepresentation of metrical poetry.

In general, the Britannica definition presents meter as a kind of prison from which it is beneficial to escape. However, meter is not an imposed restriction on expression like the decision to write a lipogram (a piece of writing that deliberately avoids the use of one or more specific letters [Stein and Urdang 1967, s. v. "lipogram"]). An imposed restriction would simply be an academic curiosity, but meter (as well as rhyme) holds a natural appeal to most human brains (Obermeier et al. 2013). This appeal derives from the fact that meter is a rhythm pattern built of sound alternations and is thus a form of music akin to note-free percussion (which is, notably, not the same thing as the drone of a metronome). In fact, through the late nineteenth century, the terms "poem" and "song" were used interchangeably in many cases (cf. Longfellow 1893: 348-349, Braxton 1993: 4-5, Cary and Cary 1884: preface) and they continued to be interchanged in some situations at least through the middle of the twentieth century (cf. Jackson 2013: 5-6, 77, 81, 152-153, 253, 264-265 and Rampersad and Roessel 1995: 46, 214, 451). Music is not a deliberate restriction on verbal expression. Music is another level of expression that a poet or songwriter attempts to advance at the same time as the meaning of their words. The only restriction on expression involved in the process of writing a metrical poem or a song comes from the fact that it is more difficult to say two things at once than one. Expressing an idea in words is more difficult when you are simultaneously trying to speak in the pure language of beauty: music. Meter should not be viewed as an artificial restriction on expression but an additional level of expression that can, in theory, exist without the use of meaningful sentences (think of scat jazz).

Additionally, there are several *particular* elements of the Britannica definition of Free Verse that imply a misrepresentation of metrical verse. One problematic element comes from the assertion that meter is one of the most abstract forms of rhythm. Stress, the basis of English meter, is much less abstract than phrases, sentences, and paragraphs. Stress in most dialects of English is realized through three straightforward, mechanically measurable qualities of a syllable: a stressed syllable is louder, longer, and higher-pitched than the syllables immediately adjacent to it (O'Grady et al. 2010: 45). Phrase and sentence structure are, on the other hand, much less clear in nature and their nature is consequently subject to much more controversy among linguists (cf. Carnie 2013, Hoffman and Trousdale 2013, O'Grady et al. 2010: Ch. 5, and Ritt 2004: 144-150). And paragraphs are not a property of language (which is an auditory phenomenon) at all — they are simply a visual tool for organizing long pieces of writing and writing, as every Linguistics 101 student learns, instead of being a part of language, is simply a tool for recording it (O'Grady et al. 2010: 545, Rogers 2005: 1-2). Another problematic element in the Britannica definition is the use of words like "regular" and "steady" to imply that metrical poetry cannot vary in rhythm almost at all. In practice, many poems, even those in traditional forms, vary the number of metrical feet from line to line or the types of feet within each line to create complex patterns. Both traditional ballad meter and limerick meter employ inconsistent line lengths (cf. Finch and Oliver 2015: 131-151 and Legman 1969) and, in sapphic stanzas, more than one type of foot is required *within* each line (Finch and Oliver 2015: 213-228). And, though this is an issue of the regularity of rhyme and not meter, it bears mentioning that a rhyming poem does not need to present a predictable rhyme scheme. ("Paul Revere's Ride" by Henry Wadsworth Longfellow, for example, while being thoroughly metrical and consistently rhyming, has no predictability in its rhyme distribution [cf. Longfellow 1893: 207-209].) There is an enormous amount of flexibility in the use of meter and rhyme when they are viewed as additional forms of expression advanced simultaneously with word-based meaning, rather than as arbitrary restrictions. Additionally, a final problematic element in the Britannica definition is the use of the phrases "the modern idiom" and "more casual tonality" both of which are misleading. The stress pattern of English has not changed substantially since the English Stress Rule (ESR) (and the subsequent changes its rise prompted) became dominant over the Old English Stress Rule (OESR) around five hundred years ago (Díaz-Vera 2013), so, in terms of stress-based meter, the "modern idiom" is not much different from the idiom of Shakespeare. And, while it is true that, in the English-speaking world, the past two centuries have seen a growth in alignment between the styles of poetic writing and casual speech (cf. Hollander 1993a and 1993b and Hass et al. 2000a and 2000b), there have always been casual varieties of English (as can be observed in, for example, the Mother Goose nursery rhymes [cf. *Mother Goose's Nursery Rhymes* 1877], which are centuries old [*Encyclopaedia Britannica* 2023, s. v. "Mother Goose"]) because there have always been casual situations, so the English of the present day as a whole does not exhibit a "more casual tonality" than the English of any other period. It is in fact, entirely possible to write completely metrical poems in a casual style (the light verse poems of Yip Harburg, Ogden Nash, and Dr. Seuss are clear examples, as are all the [often emotionally heavy] "dialect" poems of the late nineteenth and early twentieth centuries [cf. all or parts of Harburg 2006, Smith 2007, Geisel 1991, Riley 1993, Braxton 1993, Service 1940, Guest 1934, Honey 2006, Wilson 2000, Maxwell 2004, and Rampersad and Roessel 1995]) (cf. also below). Metrical poetry is not inherently formal in style and it does not have to sound unnatural. All in all, metrical poetry is not rooted in abstract qualities, is not restricted in expression, is not inherently rigid in form, is not antiquated in nature, and does not need to employ a high social register. These qualities may be associated with metrical poetry by some people, but they have never truly characterized it. And no poet today should be deterred from writing in meter (or rhyme) because of misconceptions. Ultimately, since they are fundamentally different forms of art, there is no more reason for Free Verse and metrical verse to compete for prestige and bookshelf space than there is for short stories and novels to do so and definitions like the one presented in *The Encyclopaedia Britannica* pick a fight that does not need to be fought.

<u>Subject Matter and Style</u>
By the time I was first taught to write poetry in elementary school during the late 1990s and early 2000s, there were already strong notions about what kind of subject matter was appropriate for poetry. I was started on short pieces of Free Verse (which, by that point, had succeeded in its rebellion against the metrical straw man it so deplored and had become the new establishment form of poetic writing) and the other students and I were consistently encouraged to write honest confessions of emotion, vivid descriptions of evocative scenes, and (occasionally) brief philosophical reflections. The length of our work was always supposed to be short and the subject matter was always supposed to be emotionally heavy. It wasn't until years later that I discovered that such limitations only began to become normalized a few centuries ago and only solidified as expectations during the latter part of the twentieth century.

In the early twentieth century, Langston Hughes proclaimed that "Poetry should treat/ Of lofty things" (Rampersad and Roessel 1995: 74), but he wrote that in a poem with the cynical title "Formula," so his awareness of the expectation should not necessarily be confused with advocacy. In contrast to Hughes's observation, however, one can observe that the definitions of the words "poem" and "poetry" in Samuel Johnson's classic dictionary from the eighteenth century contain no reference to any restriction on subject matter (or length or rhetorical style) (cf. below, where the edition is, however, from the early nineteenth century). In fact, tracing dictionary definitions of the words "poem" and "poetry" through the past few centuries provides insight into the shifting expectations of the subject matter, length, and rhetorical style of poetry that have taken us from a no-rules approach to the limitations imposed by my elementary school teachers. The following are several dictionary definitions of "poem" and/or "poetry" from dictionaries of various ages (formatting standardized by me):

A Table Alphabeticall (Robert Cawdrey, 1604):

- *Poeme* — verses of a poet.

(Cawdrey 2006, s. v. "poeme")

An Universal Etymological English Dictionary (Nathan Bailey, 1763):

- *Poem* — A piece of poetry, a composition in verse.
- *Poetry* — The art of making verses.

(Bailey 1763, s. v. "poem," "poetry")

A Dictionary of the English Language (Samuel Johnson and Henry John Todd, 1818):

- *Poem* — The work of a poet; a metrical composition.

- *Poetry* — 1. Metrical composition; the art or practice of writing poems 2. Poems; poetical pieces.

(Johnson 1994, s. v. "poem," "poetry")

American Dictionary of the English Language (Noah Webster, 1828):

• *Poem* — 1. A metrical composition; a composition in which the verses consist of certain measures, whether in blank verse or in rhyme; as the *poems* of Homer or of Milton; opposed to *prose*. 2. This term is also applied to some compositions in which the language is that of excited imagination; as the *poems* of Ossian.

• *Poetry* — 1. Metrical composition; verse; as heroic *poetry*; dramatic *poetry*; lyric or Pindaric *poetry*. 2. The art or practice of composing in verse. 3. Poems; poetical composition. 4. This term is also applied to the language of excited imagination and feeling.

(Webster 1995, s. v. "poem," "poetry")

The Oxford Universal Dictionary (1944):

• *Poem* — 1. The work of a poet, a metrical composition; a composition of words, expressing facts, thoughts, or feelings in poetical form; a piece of poetry. b. *transf.* Applied to a composition which, without the form, has some quality or qualities in common with poetry. 2. *fig.* Something (other than a composition of words) of a nature or quality akin to or likened to that of poetry.

• *Poetry* — 1. In obsolete senses: i. Equivalent to Medieval Latin *poetria* in sense of an *ars poetica*. ii. Fable, fiction. 2. In existing use:. i. The art or work of the poet. a. Composition in verse or metrical language. b. The product of this art as a form of literature; the writings of a poet or poets; poems collectively or generally; verse. (As opposed to *prose*). c. The expression of beautiful or elevated thought, imagination, or feeling, in appropriate language, such as language containing a rhythmical element and having usually a metric form. d. Extended to creative art in general (*rare*). ii. *pl.* Pieces of poetry; poems collectively (*rare*). 3. *fig.* Something compared to poetry; poetical quality, spirit, or feeling. 4. A class in Roman Catholic schools and colleges intermediate between *Syntax* and *Rhetoric.*

(Little et al. 1964, s. v. "poem," "poetry")

The Random House Dictionary of the English Language (1967):

- *Poem* — 1. A composition in verse, especially one that is characterized by a highly developed artistic form and by the use of heightened language and rhythm to express an intensely imaginative interpretation of the subject. 2. Composition which, though not in verse, is characterized by great beauty of language or thought. 3. Something having qualities that are suggestive of or likened to those of poetry.

- *Poetry* — 1. The art of rhythmical composition, written or spoken, for exciting pleasure by beautiful, imaginative, or elevated thoughts. 2. Literary work in metrical form; verse. 3. Prose with poetic qualities. 4. Poetic qualities however manifested. 5. Poetic spirit or feeling. 6. Something suggestive of or likened to poetry.

(Stein and Urdang 1967, s. v. "poem," "poetry")

Webster's Seventh New Collegiate Dictionary (1971):

- *Poem* — 1. A composition in verse. 2. A piece of poetry communicating to the reader the sense of a complete experience. 3. A creation, experience, or object likened to a poem.

- *Poetry* — 1. a. Metrical writing: verse. b. The productions of a poet: poems. 2. Writing that formulates a concentrated imaginative awareness of experience in language chosen and arranged to create a specific emotional response through meaning, sound, and rhythm. 3. a. A quality that stirs the imagination. b. A quality of spontaneity and grace.

(*Webster's Seventh New Collegiate Dictionary* 1971, s. v. "poem," "poetry")

The American Heritage Dictionary of the English Language, New Collegiate Edition (Morris 1980):

- *Poem* — 1. A composition designed to convey a vivid and imaginative sense of experience, characterized by the use of condensed language, chosen for its sound and suggestive power as well as its meaning, and by the use of such literary techniques as structured meter, natural cadences, rhyme, or metaphor. 2. Any composition in verse rather than in prose. 3. Any literary composition written with an intensity or beauty of language more characteristic of poetry than of prose: *a prose poem.* 4. Any creation, object, or experience thought to embody the lyrical beauty or structural perfection characteristic of poetry.

- *Poetry* — 1. The art or work of a poet. 2. a. Poems regarded as forming a division of literature. b. The poetic works of a given author, group, nation, or kind. 3. Any piece of literature written in meter; verse. 4. Prose that resembles a poem in form, sound, or the like. 5. The essence of or characteristic quality possessed by a poem or poems. 6. The quality of a poem or poems, as possessed by an object, act, or experience.

(Morris 1980, s. v. "poem," "poetry")

Funk and Wagnalls Standard Desk Dictionary (1984):

- *Poem* — 1. A composition in verse, characterized by the imaginative treatment of experience and a condensed use of language. 2. Any composition in verse. 3. Any composition or work of art characterized by intensity and beauty.

- *Poetry* — 1. The art or craft of writing poems. 2. Poems collectively. 3. The quality, effect, or spirit of a poem or of anything poetic. 4. Something that is poetic.

(*Funk and Wagnalls Standard Desk Dictionary*, Vol. 2 1984, s. v. "poem," "poetry")

The first dictionary cited above, Robert Cawdrey's *A Table Alphabeticall* of 1604 was the first monolingual English dictionary ever published (Cawdrey 2006: 7), so it is clear that, from the earliest attempts at defining poetry in dictionaries and for two centuries after that (at least through the 1818 edition of Johnson's dictionary), there was no restriction on the content, length, or rhetorical style of a poem or poetry. A poem was either defined as the work of a poet (a definition which offers no real clarification) or as a metrical composition, but no limitation existed on what the subject matter or style (other than, sometimes, meter) could be. Such limitless definitions never died out, but, starting in the nineteenth century, some new definitions started to be added to the original unconstrained ones and those new definitions often aimed to narrow the realm of subject matter and rhetorical style that was appropriate for poetry. This encroachment was peripheral at first (cf. Webster 1828), but, by the middle of the twentieth century, it had become a prominent element of definitions of "poem" and "poetry" (cf. Little et al. 1944, Stein and Urdang 1967, *Webster's Seventh New Collegiate Dictionary* 1971, Morris 1980, and *Funk and Wagnalls Standard Desk Dictionary* 1984). In the past two centuries, some people have thus constructed the idea that a poem must deal in certain types of subject matter or be presented within the constraints of certain length limits (note the definitions that cite condensed language as a requirement of poetry) and rhetorical styles. But such restrictions are not a fundamental aspect of poetry and are only relatively recent impositions.

Poems can deal in any type of subject matter, be of any length, and employ any rhetorical style. Poems can be funny as well as deeply emotional, can range in length from two lines (e. g., pithy couplets) to the length of a novel (cf. epic poems), and can be plain-spoken as well as highly formal and stylized. No natural limitation exists. The past two centuries have seen a narrowing of subject matter, accepted lengths, and rhetorical style, but modern poets do not need to constrain their work in these domains. The path forward in poetry, in fact, almost certainly lies in returning to an unlimited definition of what topics, lengths, and styles poetry can deal in because, otherwise, the creative options will run out. A poet, like any writer, should try to write something worth reading, but that is the only real restriction on their art in terms of content, length, tone, and word choice.

Paul Laurence Dunbar, one of the preeminent black poets of American history and, in my opinion, one of the poets whose work is most consistently of good quality, wrote both serious and humorous poems and wrote poems in both a highly formal standard style and in extreme forms of vernacular English (including his local Ohio dialect and the African American English of his time) (cf. Braxton 1993). And, importantly, Dunbar's choice of levity or gravity in his subject matter did not correspond to his choice of formality in style as can be seen by comparing the following of his poems: "Weltschmerz" (serious content, formal tone), "Theology," (humorous content, formal tone), "Long Ago" (serious content, vernacular dialect), and "Possum" (humorous content, vernacular dialect) (Braxton 1993: 220-221, 106, 192-193, 141-142). When considering the potential range of seriousness, rhetorical style, and dialect choice and the vast possibilities of mixing and matching the different variations of the three, the modern poet can learn a lot from Dunbar. And one should never forget that a poem can run for many thousands of words and tell a story, as do Layamon's *Brut* (cf. Madden 1847), Geoffrey Chaucer's *The Canterbury Tales* (cf. Robinson 1957: 1-265), John Lydgate's *Troy Book* (cf. Bergen 1906 and 1908), Edmund Spenser's *The Faerie Queene* (cf. Roche and O'Donnell 1978), Sir Walter Scott's *Marmion* (cf. Robertson 1904: 89-206), Henry Wadsworth Longfellow's *The Song of Hiawatha* (cf. Longfellow 1893: 113-164), and Lord Tennyson's *Idylls of the King* (cf. Gray 1996).

Conclusion

Ultimately, it is my hope that the art of poetry will enjoy a resurgence in popularity in the coming decades and I believe that one of the best ways to facilitate such a resurgence will be for poets to bear in mind the two main points of this essay: First, meter, rhyme, and other sound effects can be employed in infinite combinations, are not inherently restrictive, and offer poets ways of expressing themselves musically. And, second, a poet should not feel an obligation to restrict the subject matter, length, or rhetorical style of their poems in any way. With these considerations in mind, modern poets have unlimited possibilities for creativity and their work can usher in a renaissance of poetry in the twenty-first century. The future is ours for the inventing and there are many ways to move forward. Let us take full advantage of the possibilities.

Benjamin Cannicott Shavitz
New York, NY
June, 2023

References

Bailey, Nathan. *An Universal Etymological English Dictionary*, 20th ed. London, United Kingdom: n. p.

Bergen, Henry, ed. *Lydgate's Troy Book*, Vol. 1. London, United Kingdom: Early English Text Society, 1906.

Bergen, Henry, ed. *Lydgate's Troy Book*, Vol. 2. London, United Kingdom: Early English Text Society, 1908.

Braxton, Joanne M., ed. *The Collected Poetry of Paul Laurence Dunbar*. Charlottesville, VA and London, United Kingdom: University of Virginia Press, 1993.

Carnie, Andrew. *Syntax: A Generative Introduction*, 3rd ed. Malden, MA: Wiley-Blackwell, 2013.

Cary, Alice and Phoebe Cary. *The Poetical Works of Alice and Phoebe Cary*, Household ed. Boston, MA: Houghton, Mifflin, and Company, 1884.

Cawdrey, Robert. *The First English Dictionary 1604: Robert Cawdrey's A Table Alphabetical*. Oxford, United Kingdom: Bodleian Library, 2006.

Díaz-Vera, Javier E. "Stress Change and Phonological Variation in Early Modern English, British and American." *Jezikoslovlje* 14, no. 1 (2013): 33-46.

Encyclopaedia Britannica, s. v. "Free Verse." Chicago: Encyclopaedia Britannica, 2023.
https://www.britannica.com/art/free-verse (accessed June 6, 2023).

Encyclopaedia Britannica, s. v. "Mother Goose." Chicago: Encyclopaedia Britannica, 2023.
https://www.britannica.com/topic/Mother-Goose-fictional-character (accessed June 7, 2023).

Finch, Annie and Alexander Oliver, eds. *Measure for Measure: An Anthology of Poetic Meters (Everyman's Library Pocket Poets)*. New York/London/Toronto: Alfred A. Knopf, 2015.

Funk and Wagnalls Standard Desk Dictionary, Vol. 2. New York, NY: Harper and Row, 1984.

Geisel, Theodor. *Six by Seuss: A Treasury of Dr. Seuss Classics*. New York, NY: Random House, 1991.

Gray, J. M., ed. *Alfred, Lord Tennyson: Idylls of the King*. London, United Kingdom and New York, NY: Penguin, 1996.

Guest, Edgar A. *Collected Verse of Edgar A. Guest*. Chicago, IL: Contemporary Books, 1934.

Harburg, Edgar Yipsel. *Rhymes for the Irreverent*. Madison, WI: The Freedom from Religion Foundation, 2006.

Hass, Robert, John Hollander, Carolyn Kizer, Nathaniel Mackey, and Marjorie Perloff, eds. *American Poetry: The Twentieth Century*, Vol. 1. New York, NY: The Library of America, 2000a.

Hass, Robert, John Hollander, Carolyn Kizer, Nathaniel Mackey, and Marjorie Perloff, eds. *American Poetry: The Twentieth Century*, Vol. 2. New York, NY: The Library of America, 2000b.

Hoffman, Thomas and Graeme Trousdale, eds. *The Oxford Handbook of Construction Grammar*. Oxford, United Kingdom: Oxford University Press, 2013.

Hollander, John, ed. *American Poetry: The Nineteenth Century*, Vol. 1. New York, NY: The Library of America, 1993a.

Hollander, John, ed. *American Poetry: The Nineteenth Century*, Vol. 2. New York, NY: The Library of America, 1993b.

Honey, Maureen, ed. *Shadowed Dreams: Women's Poetry of the Harlem Renaissance*, 2nd ed., revised and expanded. New Brunswick, NJ and London, United Kingdom: Rutgers University Press, 2006.

Jackson, Major, ed. *Countee Cullen: Collected Poems*. New York, NY: The Library of America, 2013.

Johnson, Samuel. *A Dictionary of the English Language*, abridged from H. J. Todd's Corrected and Enlarged Quarto ed. by Alexander Chalmers, Barnes and Noble reprint ed. New York, NY: Barnes and Noble Books, 1994.

Legman, G., ed. *The Limerick: 1700 Examples, with Notes, Variants and Index*. New York, NY: Bell Publishing, 1969.

Little, William, H. M. Fowler, and J. Coulson, eds. *The Oxford Universal Dictionary on Historical Principles*, 3rd ed. revised with addenda by C. T. Onions. Oxford, United Kingdom: Oxford University Press, 1964.

Longfellow, Henry Wadsworth. *The Complete Poetical Works of Longfellow*. Boston, MA: Houghton Mifflin, 1893.

Madden, Sir Frederic, ed. *Layamon's Brut, Chronicle of Britain: A Poetical Semi-Saxon Paraphrase of the Brut of Wace* (in three volumes). London, United Kingdom: The Society of Antiquaries of London, 1847.

Maxwell, William J., ed. *Complete Poems: Claude McKay*. Urbana, IL and Chicago, IL: University of Illinois Press, 2004.

Morris, William, ed. *The American Heritage Dictionary of the English Language*, New Collegiate ed. Boston, MA: Houghton Mifflin, 1980.

Mother Goose's Nursery Rhymes: A Collection of Alphabets, Rhymes, Tales, and Jingles. London, United Kingdom and New York, NY: George Routledge and Sons, 1877.

Obermeier, Christian, Winfried Menninghaus, Martin von Koppenfels, Tim Raettig, Maren Schmidt-Kassow, Sascha Otterbein, and Sonja A. Kotz. "Aesthetic and Emotional Effects of Meter and Rhyme in Poetry." *Frontiers in Psychology* 4 (2013): article 10.

O'Grady, William, John Archibald, Mark Aronoff, and Janie Rees-Miller, eds. *Contemporary Linguistics: An Introduction*, 6th ed. Boston and New York: Bedford/ St. Martin's, 2010.

Rampersad, Arnold and David Roessel, eds. *The Collected Poems of Language Hughes*, First Vintage Classics ed. New York, NY: Vintage Classics, 1995.

Riley, James Whitcomb. *The Complete Poetical Works of James Whitcomb Riley.* Bloomington, IN and Indianapolis, IN: Indiana University Press, 1993.

Ritt, Nikolaus. *Selfish Sounds and Linguistic Evolution: A Darwinian Approach to Language Change.* Cambridge, United Kingdom: Cambridge University Press, 2004.

Robertson, J. Logie, ed. *The Poetical Works of Sir Walter Scott.* London, United Kingdom: Oxford University Press, 1904.

Robinson, F. N., ed. *The Works of Geoffrey Chaucer*, 2nd ed. Boston, MA: Houghton Mifflin, 1957.

Roche, Thomas P., Jr. and C. Patrick O'Donnell, Jr., eds. *Edmund Spenser: The Faerie Queene.* London, United Kingdom and New York, NY: Penguin Books, 1978.

Rogers, Henry. *Writing Systems: A Linguistic Approach.* Malden, MA: Blackwell, 2005.

Service, Robert. *Collected Poems of Robert Service.* New York, NY: G. P. Putnam's Sons, 1940.

Smith, Linell Nash, ed. *The Best of Ogden Nash.* Chicago, IL: Ivan R. Dee, 2007.

Stein, Jess and Laurence Urdang, eds. *The Random House Dictionary of the English Language*, Unabridged ed. New York, NY: Random House, 1967.

Webster, Noah. *Noah Webster's First Edition of An American Dictionary of the English Language*, Facsimile ed. San Francisco, CA: Foundation for American Christian Education, 1995.

Webster's Seventh New Collegiate Dictionary. Springfield, MA: G. and C. Merriam Company, 1971.

Wilson, Sondra Kathryn, ed. *James Weldon Johnson: Complete Poems*. London, United Kingdom and New York, NY: Penguin Books, 2000.